A DISEASE, A JOURNEY, AND ONE

Telly Stories

Dedication to those with a similar Diagnosis

This story was written because there are more and more individuals being diagnosed with Rhuematoid Arthritis or another Auto-immune disease. It is an extremely stressfull disorder, one I do not wish even on my enemies (if I have any). I really just wanted to reach out to everyone who is going through this struggle, including the family members of those with a diagnosis. I honestly believe that if we come together, talk about our frustrations, express our sincere concerns, heart breaks, and failures with those loved ones that we trust wholeheartedly that we can not only get through another day in this struggle but we then can reach out to others in an effort to help them as well.

So, in closing this little section I want to wish all of you well, and may God Bless each and every one of you.

About the Book

A Disease, a Journey, and One was written with an attempt to relate to readers, find hope, and comfort that One is not alone in the battle against diseases. I was diagnosed with Rheumatoid Arthritis in 2012, some eight years ago. It has not gotten any better or easier in understanding the how or why, but I have learned a few things about the disease and myself along the way. My hope is that somehow, I am able to inspire others, bring some peace or comfort to sufferers and their families, and maybe shed some of the feelings of being so alone with all that diseases entail.

Table of Contents

                                          Page

Chapter One: Diagnosis   4

Chapter Two: Initial Response to Diagnosis   13

Chapter Three: Mourning self/loss   17

Chapter Four: Everyone has advice   19

Chapter Five: Accept or Ask for specific help 22

Chapter Six: How I Cope   25

CHAPTER ONE: DIAGNOSIS

When I got up this morning my hands were a little swollen and hurt mildly. I put on my Cafeteria Aide uniform and headed out to go serve breakfast at our local Elementary school, like I did every morning. I arrived at the school and began preparing trays of food for the children. I love this job I thought as the children would come into the cafeteria one by one grabbing a milk and a tray of food. Some children were still tired, and others were wired, ready for the day to begin but, all would smile and thank me for doing my job.

As the crowd of children began to eat, and time for eating breakfast would then end I began cleaning my station and putting food away. As I began the breakfast count (how many children were served), I notice my left hand feels more swollen and painful to hold the pencil to write. As I look at my hand (as if to say "What is wrong with you"), I begin feeling frightened. My wedding ring seems to be disappearing into my finger, the swelling is increasing! I run some cold water over my hand for a few minutes in hopes that the swelling will decrease. But, after five minutes or so nothing changes. Now I begin to think, "I need to get the ring off!" Somehow, I am thinking the ring is squeezing the finger. I grab some ice, put it in a baggy and on my finger, after ten minutes...no change. At this point my finger is consuming the ring on my finger, I really need the ring to come off. So, I call my boss to explain to her what is going on and reassure her it was not a "work-related" injury but, that I will need to go to the emergency room to get the ring cut off; so I will not be able to return to work this afternoon to serve lunch. She reassures me that my shift will be covered and tells me to go now. I then call my husband (we try to have lunch together daily at home when we can), to let him know what is going on, he decides to take me to the emergency room.

When we arrive and sign all the paperwork, they bring me some ice in a container to attempt to reverse some of the swelling. Apparently, my body decided it did not want to respond to their attempts either so after approximately 15 minutes they decided they needed to cut it off...quickly. Of course, they asked me what I did, "Did you smash your hand at work or what?" They were in disbelief that there was absolutely no injury or any thing that "triggered" the swelling. As the doctor came in, he asked the same question, then asked has this happened before? I explained that my bones had been hurting more lately, with slight swelling in my feet, knees, hips, and hands but nothing like this swelling. He took notes then right away grabbed the equipment to begin cutting my ring at the underside-middle of my ring. I began screaming, kicking the legs to the hospital bed, and crying. The equipment used had to be slid under the ring which made the ring plunge into my skin more! After the cut, they put my husband on one side and doctor on the other side of the ring to attempt to pull the rings' sides out wide enough to come off my swollen finger. Of course, my finger was too swollen, and this approach did not work. So, now just like they had just done, the doctor had to slide the device under the ring and over the finger to make another cut. Screaming and kicking in pain, the doctor once again employs my husband to pull on a side of the ring to pull it off. Finally, it is off, but the finger is throbbing. The doctor says, "this is the worst I've seen a finger swell up over a ring!", which does not make me feel any better. My husband takes a picture of my finger in disbelief that my finger has an exact imprint of the design of my ring's underside. Due to the severity of swelling, the doctor orders an x-ray to eliminate the possibility of a broken bone or other damage. After waiting for the results, I am told all is clear, so I am cleared to leave with a recommendation to get a referral from my physician for a rheumatologist as soon as possible.

My next step was to follow up with my regular physician and to put in for a referral request to a rheumatologist. It seemed as though it took forever, however a couple weeks after my E.R. visit the local rheumatologist wanted blood tests done before considering me as a patient. When my blood work came back negative for an RA factor, ANA, and gout; the local rheumatologist doctor rejected my request to see him. My physician's office said the only options remaining are out of town specialists. I agreed to see one as I needed answers as to why in the world my hands would just swell up for no apparent reason. I was scheduled for a month out and pondered what the visit would entail. My first visit to see my rheumatologist was scary, I had no idea what to expect, what kind of tests would be done, and if I would leave this office with an answer.

The specialist began with family history questions to compare with potentially inherited conditions. Then she grabbed my hands to look them over (some swelling was present), she had me place the tops of my wrists together, with my hands pointed down and asked me what I felt. Then she did the reflex test on my knees along with a few other strange testing maneuvers.

do to me long term, what are other things that could happen? How damaged is my body? What parts of my body are currently affected, and will that change? I quickly realized that although "it had a name" and my initial query was answered that now I had more questions. So, I began researching what this Rheumatoid arthritis is and what are the causes. To my surprise I found simply put that Rheumatoid arthritis is an auto-immune disease with no known cause. Of course, that was not good enough for me, so I searched more. There are speculations that a dramatic event has triggered the R.A., or that it is inherited but, there is little known for certain what causes R.A. I did find that this disease is life-altering in the sense that I cannot do things as I used to, they need some modifying. For instance, I used to sweep and then mop the floor by getting on my hands and knees to scrub the floor... I cannot do that anymore, it hurts way too bad. I also used to move the furniture to vacuum behind it, then move it all back...cannot do that anymore either. As these realizations came to light and finding out as much as I can about this disease and what it could mean for my future, I began to become saddened.

still get things completed. It may sound like depression but, realizing how broken you feel, lost, or helpless; and then talking about it to a trusted loved one, and crying allows for one chapter of your life to close but, another to open up to you. The person you choose to open up to, should not only be understanding and compassionate, but they need to have knowledge of this life-altering disease.

Chapter Four: Everyone has advice

While this will most likely be welcomed, initially. It will become confusing and frustrating. Remember, that your doctor knows medicine not your body's response to the illness or the medicine given. This is important to keep in mind because your loved ones will have concerns that "your doctor doesn't know what they are doing, giving you medicines that makes you sick, or breaks your other organs instead of treating your pain!" While family means well, they often want to treat your Rheumatoid Arthritis, like arthritis. Some suggestions may help, like heating or cooling pads, and anti-inflammatory natural supplements but, some suggestions like "if you exercise more it will help loosen your joints", may aggravate the joints more. Diet and exercise are important regardless of any illness but, running and jumping put more impact pressure on the joints, and some routines may do your body more harm than good, so it is important to ask your doctor for advice before beginning a diet or exercise plan. Each of us are completely different in our response to medicine, exercise, herbal remedies, etc. So even though there is massive amounts of information and research on what helps with your symptoms, what may help me may not work so well for you.

A family's
Love™
is forever

This Photo by Unknown Author is licensed under CC BY-SA-NC

CHAPTER 5: ACCEPT OR ASK FOR SPECIFIC HELP

Us as humans want to help those we care about and want help when we need it. However, when a loved one wants to help too much you may feel like a burden or as if they are treating you like a cripple. On the other side to that, you may be feeling as though you are not getting enough help. I fell into this area that either too much or too little help would hurt my feelings and make me angrier at my inability to function the way I always had. So, I had to express to my loved ones how and when/where I needed assistance. I had to learn to accept the help given and feel relieved and grateful instead of ashamed. I had to learn to forgive myself for needing the assistance, for not being able to do certain things anymore, or for having to change the way I do things. I also had to learn how to talk about my feelings. These are all so important for your health, relationships, and well-being.

Sometimes, I just wanted to have a big Help button to push. Rather than asking for help. I realized what was happening in not such a wonderful way in this. I was getting so upset with myself for not being able to get up form my chair (to grab a drink, while my husband made dinner), that my actions made my husband think I was upset with him for not being available to help me up. So, he got angry. It was not until we talked it out that I realized just how important my words were. Now, when I attempt to do things on my own and cannot; I speak it. I simply ask, "Can you open my water bottle, I just can't get it"? Or whatever it may be. I attempt it (so I don't feel like I'm giving up on myself) but if I cannot do whatever it is and I have someone around me I ask for the help and express my aggravation with words rather than noises or faces which could be taken very differently or wrong.

Chapter 6: How I cope

First and foremost, God. While this is not a religious book it is certainly an individual conviction and profession of faith. Without my faith in God, I would have had no Will to push past any and all of the enclosed realizations, pain, sorrow, or sadness. I would have sunk into a pit of darkness without hope, without love for myself, and without love for others. My hatred for myself would have consumed me to the point of destruction of self, my marriage, and friendships. God not only held me above all of this but, he held my husband safe in His loving arms and opened both of our eyes to see, this to be yet another attempt of the evil one to destroy all that we hold dear. There are still times that I find it difficult to accept and get angry at myself and my limitations. I become angry at my body for being "broken" is what my husband and I jokingly call it. However, above all God has gifted me with the knowledge of self-talk. In psychology terms it is known as Cognitive-behavioral therapy (CBT). Simply put, I begin hearing these negative thoughts entering my mindabout my limitations, pain, and the frustration it brings within me. Then I begin replacing or rebutting these negative thoughts with positive thoughts instead. It took practice, this did not come easy. It began with simple things such as: rather than using my thumb and first finger to open a water bottle, I use the palm of my hand. I began figuring out different ways to do things. I take breaks in between doing a sink full of dishes or vacuuming. So, negative thoughts would be replaced with things like: "I may not be able to do all of the dishes at once, but I can still get them all done". Another one is "For now, I may have a lot of pain when going from a sitting position to standing, but I can still stand and walk down my hallway to the restroom". The more I use this strategy the better (emotionally) I feel about my limitations. I often remind myself I may not be able to do certain things that are too taxing on my body but, there are many things I can still do if I just have patience with myself. I can no longer work outside of the home to help my husband with the bills, so I do more of the chores throughout his work week so that he does not have to worry about doing those over the weekend. Instead he and I can actually relax, watch a movie, or go enjoy time out of the house together. It may be difficult, financially at times. However, the thought then enters my mind "God will not let us starve". He will provide for us as we need it, He always has and always will.

All you have to do it cry out to Him.

BOOKS BY THIS AUTHOR

Silly Dreams

Children's book, assisting Lana a little girl who has scary dreams until her Grandmother makes up a silly story in hopes that Lana will have silly dreams rather than her typical scary dreams.

Lana's First Trip To The Beach

Lana takes her first trip to the beach with her family. Can you guess some of the exciting things she sees?

Lana And The Covid-19 Virus

Lana's perspective on handling or struggling through the daily changes that have happened in her world since this virus came to her town. How her life has changed and what she has done with her family to cope.

Made in the USA
Columbia, SC
28 August 2020